Angels - For Hire

Ranjini Woodhouse

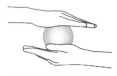

SOULJOURNEY PUBLISHING

Second Edition
Published by: Souljourney Publishing
May 2012

ISBN: 978-0-9570251-1-0

First edition published by Souljourney Publishing

You may contact the author through her website:
www.souljourney.co.uk

Cover design Copyright © 2011 James Woodhouse

Interior Design and layout by James Woodhouse

DEDICATION

To God and the angels
who are my constant companions
and my spiritual support system.

To my husband John
and my children
James and Zoë
for your loving support.

CONTENTS

GRANDMA USED TO READ FROM THE BIBLE

"And there appeared an angel unto him from
heaven strengthening him."
Luke 22:43

"For He shall give His angels charge over thee
to keep thee in all ways.
They shall bear thee in their hands, lest thou
dash thy foot against a stone."
Psalm 91:11-12

"There is joy in the presence of the angels of
God."
Luke 15:10

'And the angel said unto them
"Fear not: for behold,
I bring you good tidings of
great joy which shall be to all people." '
Luke 2: 10

WHY I BELIEVE IN ANGELS?

My belief in angels started when I was about three or four years old. Even if my parents went out for a short while, I would miss them, be afraid and cry. I recall that on these occasions my maternal grandma would hug me and say, "There is nothing to be afraid of because God has sent his angels to watch over you."

One day, when I was about five years old, I realised that my grandma was not around. When I asked my parents where she was, they said she had gone to heaven to be with God and his angels. I was sad and missed her physical presence however I knew she would continue to ask the angels to protect me. Soon after I had diphtheria and was in an isolation ward. Each time I felt scared and lonely because my parents or grandma were not around to give me a hug and tell me not to be afraid, I would remember my mother's and grandma's comforting words and would call to the angels for help. Within a few seconds my feeling of fear reduced and a sense of calm came over me and I knew that the angels were with me.

As I grew up, I wanted to fit in with society's concept of how life should be and relegated my belief in angels to the back of my mind. My thoughts were if others knew about it, I would be called weird, strange or even crazy. As time went by, I realised that I was like a zombie, doing things that were expected of me. I had lost my identity and the meaning in my life. To find the real me again I started reading self-help books and learnt reiki and other healing modalities but I was still not happy within. One day, after teaching a reiki class, I was in the garden and spoke aloud. "There must be something more that I can do to find the real me."

A few days later, I started noticing number sequences such as 444, 111, 422, 737 on digital clocks and on car number plates. I asked a friend if these number sequences meant something and his reply was, "They are angel messages," but he had no idea what they signified. At the same time I was hearing about books on angels and I slowly started realising that there were others in the world who also believed in their existence and that I was not the odd one out. As my thoughts turned towards the angels I felt an overwhelming sense of calm and peace, just like I felt when I was a child. This was the angels reminding me of their presence.

One day while I was out shopping my attention was drawn to a bookshop and found myself in front of the "Mind, Body, Spirit" section. As I scanned the bookshelf, the book "Healing with the Angels" by Doreen Virtue, literally fell out. I picked it and let it fall open; it opened on the page that had number sequences and the angelic messages. I immediately bought the book came home and read it from cover to cover within a day.

To build my confidence to ask for help from the angels, I read many other such books and attended a few courses facilitated by Doreen Virtue and Kimberly Marooney and yet I was a little sceptical about the vast amount of assistance the angels offer us. I started asking them for guidance for simple things, like a parking space, or help with what to cook for the family for dinner each day, and as I received their assistance I was pleasantly surprised. My scepticism slowly disappeared and I now call upon them for assistance with both little things and big things.

I have faced many challenges and traumatic situations over the past few years and during these times I was very agitated, upset, and unable to think clearly. I turned to the angels and kept repeating, "Angels, please help. I don't know what to do." Within a few seconds, I felt calm, was able to think clearly and immediately deal with the situation at hand.

I now call on the angels on a daily basis. I am no longer afraid that people may think I am weird or crazy and I speak openly about my belief in angels. I would like to share with you how I request angelic help to make personal changes, build trust and faith in God and myself.

1. WHO ARE THE ANGELS?

Different cultures, races, and religions believe in the existence of heavenly beings. In Judaism, Islam, Hinduism, Buddhism and Zoroastrianism they are referred to as benevolent, heavenly, celestial or shining ones, who are messengers of God and act as intermediaries between heaven and earth. All religions believe that heavenly beings are powerful thought forms of God's unconditional love. They carry all the different aspects of God. All the abilities and talents of the heavenly beings are from God and therefore they are continuously connected to God in praise and gratitude. When you see the word God, you may replace it with Divine Source, Universe, Allah, Shiva, Higher Power, Eternal Light, Great White Spirit, or whatever designation you are comfortable with.

Angel means a messenger in Greek and in Latin Angelus refers to angels. Angelus is derived from the opening words of a Latin devotional prayer, 'Angelus Domini nuntiavit Marice,' (the angel of the Lord declared unto Mary....). Angels as messengers of God are an integral part in the Christian approach and terminology. In Islam, angels are referred to as maleks or farishtas and are believed to be messengers from Allah. In Judaism, malachim are messengers of God who carry out God's plan. The first five books of the Bible refer to angelic intervention, which is also mentioned in the Torah, one example being where the angels intervened when Abraham was preparing his son for sacrifice. Archangel Gabriel (hazarat Jibril) and Archangel Michael (hazarat Mikaael) are mentioned in the Bible as well as the Qur'an.

Hinduism does not specifically have any angels but has many different types of minor gods and goddesses or shining ones who act in a similar capacity to them. Buddhist philosophy too does not have any angels as understood in other religions but different schools of Buddhism have important heavenly beings referred to as devas, devatas or dharmapalas derived from pre-Buddhist cultures and religions.

Angels look past your "human faults." They are non-judgemental and non-critical. Therefore you do not need to change your religious beliefs to call on them to guide you on your spiritual or religious path. Their only focus is to love you unconditionally and to help you find your own divinity within.

Angels are always around you; therefore use the terminology that you prefer; whether angels, heavenly beings, shining ones, devas, devatas, dharmapalas, maleks, faristas, devdoots, gods or goddesses to call on them for guidance.

God is a loving parent wishing us an abundant

life. He does not want us to suffer in any way. When we incarnated we had everything we needed for an abundant life. Soon after we were born, due to cultural thinking and society's beliefs of how life should be, our egos started to grow and we became obsessed with money, status, security, material things, and forgetting why we chose to incarnate on this planet, have moved away from God.

To help you remember your life's mission for this incarnation, and to remind you of God's infinite love, situations arise in life that bring you illusions of pain and suffering. This is a call from your soul to release your pain and suffering and to awaken to your spiritual qualities of love, compassion and joy. You may not know where or how to start this process. Help is at hand. Become aware of the millions and millions of unemployed angels waiting everywhere around you, your loved ones, your house, office and garden, ready to assist you, to lighten your earthly burdens, raise your conscious awareness of your divine self and to help you to have a more satisfying relationship with God, self and others.

Angels will never try to run your life or change you. They will not intervene in any situation until you ask for help but will stay with you even if you do not call on them for assistance. This is because God gave you free will and choice to make your own decisions and act on your personal beliefs. Even when you do not follow their guidance, they will still love and support you and never withdraw from you.

Angels have their own unique special talents and abilities. Each one of you has a team of powerful angels best suited to your talents and abilities. They guide, protect, support and love you daily. God sends you extra angels when you face a traumatic situation or challenges in your life. During such times, the angels love, support and help you to heal, to find inner peace and remind you of your true divine nature, which is unconditional love.

Angels are your best friends and constant companions on your life's path. You can share your darkest and deepest thoughts and innermost feelings with them. They will listen to you without judgement or criticism, will guide, support and love you every step of the way. Angels will assist you to heal yourself from issues large or small, to shift your consciousness to your Divine aspect of your God self. They will not do your work for you, but will help you do so. For example, if you have a negative thought or feeling, call on the angels to help you find the root cause and give you clarity of that thought or feeling and help you release it. Even if you do not follow their guidance, they will still love and support you from the lowest moment of your life to the highest and never withdraw from you.

As you become aware of the presence of the angels, and call on them for help, they will increasingly reveal themselves to you. Angels live and work constantly and tirelessly, protecting and guiding humanity. They are always opening new doors to love and closing unwanted ones. When you become consciously aware of the angels they will shower you with God's pure love and light. Angels help and comfort you in every area of your life. The reason angels are able to create miracles in your life daily is because they know that God's unconditional love is everywhere and in everything. If you are sceptical about the existence of angels, that is fine. Angels believe in you and are always with you.

2. WHAT DO ANGELS LOOK LIKE?

Christians, Hindus, Muslims and Buddhists all believe that angels, gods, goddesses, devas, devatas, dharmapalas, devdoots are the essence of God's love and light; therefore they do not need a physical body or wings to fly.

Angels are vibrating energy fields; they glow in different colours, shapes and sizes. They do not have any gender; and are androgynous, that is, with both male and female qualities. They are just vast swirls of energy, with their own energy vibrations. Their specific fortes and characteristics give them strong and gentle (male) or gentle and soft (female) energy. We perceive them as male and female.

The Christian concept is the image of a human with wings and halo as depicted in Renaissance paintings. In Islam it is believed that angels do not have a physical body but may show themselves in different forms in dreams or visions.

The minor gods and goddesses in Hinduism are depicted in physical form to recognise the different aspects of God. In Buddhism devas devatas or dharmapalas are described as enormous fields of light, whereas in Tibetan Buddhism they are often depicted in physical form. Whatever religious path you follow, the belief in heavenly beings or angels is that they are messengers of God and they are always sending out love and light to the earth is a common denominator.

3. DIFFERENCE BETWEEN ANGELS, ASCENDED MASTERS AND SPIRIT GUIDES

Angels have never incarnated on earth. It is believed that a few angels chose to incarnate on earth only for a lifetime or for a specific period of time.

Ascended Masters are spiritual teachers or great prophets and they come from all cultures and religions, who once walked on this planet, they have balanced their karma, the reason for incarnating on earth, and are now enlightened beings, reunited with God. They continue to help humanity from their heavenly home. Examples of ascended masters are Jesus, Mother Mary, Quan Yin, Kuan Ti, Lanto, Mohamed, Krishna, Babaji, Shirdi Sai Baba, and Buddha.

Spirit Guides are souls that have lived many lifetimes on this planet and have gained much wisdom and continue evolving towards enlightenment. They come from different cultures and religions. They can be with you for one lifetime or for a short period while you change and evolve. When you reach the next stage of your evolution, another spirit guide best suited to your needs will appear. A spirit guide may appear as a warrior, a storyteller, a nurse and so on.

Ancestral Guides are your deceased loved ones. They could be your parents, grandparents, siblings, husband, wife, other family members, or close friends. They appear to give you reassurances if you are still grieving or to give guidance. Their messages will reflect their personalities as when they were living. They give messages relating to concerns such as when to start school, sell or buy the house, regarding your love life, health concerns or about a new addition to the family and so on. Some refer to their deceased loved ones as their guardian angels.

Soul Guides are more evolved than you and are wiser than spirit guides. The role of your soul guide is to help you and your soul group to evolve spiritually lifetime after lifetime. A soul group can be the family that you are born into, a group of friends, or people who were born at the same time under similar circumstances with similar views but may not know each other and live in different parts of the world. A soul group is always working in concert whether they are aware of it or not to bring love, light and joy to all humanity.

4. THE HIERARCHY OF ANGELS

The hierarchy of the angels has evolved through God's powerful thought forms of unconditional love. As angels are messengers of God, He has infused each angel with all of His attributes to share with humanity. The hierarchy or the order of the angels resembles the tributaries of a river. A parent river can have many tributaries yet their main function is to carry water from the source. Each angel may carry an attribute of God, with all the attributes blending together in God's unconditional love.

Ten spheres of angels are mentioned in the Jewish faith. In the Islamic faith, a set order or hierarchy exists between angels, defined by the missions and various tasks that God has empowered them with. Some scholars suggest that Islamic angels can be grouped into fourteen categories. The Hindu faith refers to 333 million gods and goddesses or aspects of God, with a hierarchical system within devas, devatas and mahadevas.

According to Dionysius the Areopagite a Christian theologian and philosopher in, his writings and teachings mentions three spheres of angels with categories of angels within each sphere.

First Sphere (Heavenly Counsellors)
Seraphim
Cherubim
Thrones

Second Sphere (Heavenly Governors)
Dominions
Virtues
Powers

Third Sphere (Heavenly Messengers)
Principalities
Archangels
Angels

As I learnt more about the angels, I found another perspective to the hierarchy of angels which departed from the traditional Christian system. As this included the influence of the Qabalah, the Qur'an and a touch of Hinduism and Buddhism, it resonates with my feelings and truths.

This hierarchy of angels is composed of:

Archangels and Lesser Archangels are more powerful than the angels. They continuously transmit unconditional love to all inhabitants of the earth. There are many bands of angels that work with the archangels. Archangel Michael and angels of mercy, Archangel Gabriel and angels of communication, Archangel Raphael and healing angels, Archangel Uriel and angels of ministration. Archangel Chamuel and the angels of love. Within the groups of angels there are different orders.

First Order Angels are the angels of love, partnership, balance, vision and gratitude. Their energies are soft and shimmering and full of love. They help you to follow the desires of your heart, find God's eternal love within you and project to others visions of the Divine.

Second Order Angels are the angels of manifestation, knowledge, communication, beauty and truth. If you are starting on a new project, these angels will help you to recognise and release your weaknesses, show you your strengths and offer clarity in order to bring your vision into fruition and follow your spiritual destiny.

Third Order Angels assist you to open your heart to God's eternal love. They help you to find the truth about your negative feelings to transform your life to find inner peace, love, wisdom and unity with your eternal self.

Fourth Order Angels help you to explore your emotional wounds conquer your lack of self-esteem, self-worth, doubt, and separation from God. When you awaken to your Divine plan and transform yourself, your daily life receives a new quality of heightened unconditional love, joy and compassion.

Golden Light Angels bring you hope, courage, mercy and peace. They help you to release intense emotions of anger, rage, doubt, worry, fear and unforgiveness providing you with opportunities for deep healing and self-growth.

Seraphim offer you power and freedom from fear of receiving God's miracles.

Cherubim shower you with Divine grace, blessings and prosperity.

Seraphim and Cherubim are very powerful angels. They have long been trying to reunite with humanity but their power and light which can be compared to fire and wind is so great that humanity has been afraid of them. Now, more and more people are becoming aware of the angelic presence, and as they release their fears are connecting with the Seraphim and Cherubim to bring love, peace, harmony and joy into this world.

Guardian Angel is your personal angel, has been with you since you first incarnated on this planet and throughout all your lifetimes, is your best friend and companion, and knows you intimately. How to call on your guardian angel for help is given in chapter 17.

5. ARCHANGELS

There are seven great archangels mentioned in religious texts, but it is believed that there are many lesser archangels. Archangels, because of their magnitude and power, have the ability to be with everyone who calls on them at the same time. Some abilities of the archangels and angels are similar but they have slightly different interests. For example, archangel Chamuel encourages self love, while angel Hadraniel awakens you to the memory of eternal love. Both archangel Ariel and angel Fortuna are angels of prosperity. Archangel Ariel is a powerful angel of nature and its prosperity while angel Fortuna brings wealth of spirit. Archangel Michael and angel Indriel together help clear toxins from your mental, emotional and physical bodies. Archangel Metatron and angel Opal both protect children.

The seven great Archangels are -

MICHAEL (He who is like God)
His chief function is to protect your spiritual destiny and assist you in fulfilling it. He also protects your body and mind and helps rid the earth and humanity of fear. He also provides guidance, direction, choice of career path and assistance with your life's purpose. He brings with him clarity, wisdom and love to make positive changes in your life.

As the angel of protection, strength and courage, Archangel Michael is your "Mr Fix It" for any and all situations that may arise in your life. No task is too big or small for him. His energy is very powerful and strong.

Colour: Royal blue with tinges of purple and gold
Crystals: Sugilite, Azurite

JOPHIEL (Beauty of God)
He helps you to consciously discover and be aware of the love and light within your soul. Archangel Jophiel's energies are very soft and gentle. He assists in beautifying your thoughts, to create, manifest and illuminate the wisdom of love within you. If you feel overwhelmed, stressful and filled with unloving thoughts or feelings, if you are in "victim mode," or know that you have allowed your ego to be in control, tell archangel Jophiel what has upset you and give him permission to intervene and to beautify your thoughts and help you refocus on love and peace.

If you are thinking of beautifying your office or house and are unsure of the best location to hang a picture or place a piece of furniture, or if you want to plant something new in your garden and not sure of the location, ask archangel Jophiel to guide you to the right spot. Archangel

Jophiel helps you to see the beauty and the love of God that is within you, around you and within others.

Colour: Deep rose pink
Crystals: Rubelite, Tourmaline (pink)

CHAMUEL (He who sees God)

Archangel Chamuel is the angel of love, tolerance, gratitude and peace. He helps build and strengthen relationships. If you are seeking out a soul mate, a new career path or your life purpose, he will guide you towards your goal. If you have been hurt, and you are suffering from a broken heart, call upon archangel Chamuel to infuse you with Divine love and energy to help mend your broken heart and find inner peace.

Archangel Chamuel is a powerful healer and leader in the angelic hierarchy, and is known as the 'Powers' who protects the world from fearful lower energies. You can call upon archangel Chamuel for comfort, protection and intervention in world events leading to world peace.

Colour: Pale Green
Crystal: Pale green fluorite

GABRIEL (God is my strength)

Archangel Gabriel is the bringer of good news, and is often depicted with a trumpet. He appeared to Mother Mary with the news of the birth of Jesus. It is believed that he watched over prophet Mohamed while he wrote the Qur'an and helped Zoroaster on his spiritual path. He is the angel of resurrection. Resurrection means to bring to life again. Thus he helps to clear negative emotions and beliefs and brings the qualities of joy, grace, and clarity into your life. When life becomes dull and routine due to fear, Archangel Gabriel will give you strength and guide you to the changes you need to make.

As an angel of communication and bearer of good news, he aids students, artists, journalists, writers, actors, astronomers and scientists. He also helps with child conception, fertility, pregnancy and adoption of children. He opens doors for spiritual growth. The energies of Archangel Gabriel are very feminine, soft, gentle and subtle yet strong and powerful.

Colour: Copper
Crystal: Copper, Citrine

RAPHAEL (God Heals)
Archangel Raphael glows a beautiful emerald green healing energy. His mission is to heal physical challenges, illness or pain. He brings instant release from suffering and nourishes the body and mind with the pure essence of spirit. He is a powerful spiritual surgeon in releasing fear from your mind and body. He works closely

with those involved in the medical profession and all therapists.

He assists those suffering from any form of addiction; it may be drugs, alcohol, food or even negative thought patterns, to overcome these habits. He brings in the qualities of healing, illumination, balance and abundance.

Archangel Raphael also helps with travel. If you intend travelling ask him to ensure a stress free, safe journey.

Colour: Emerald green
Crystal: Emerald

URIEL (God is Light)
He is the angel of illumination, ministration, peace and tranquillity, often depicted carrying a lantern. Archangel Uriel soothes conflicts and replaces them with serenity. Call on him to free yourself from fears, to break the emotional and mental chains that restrict you from moving forward on your life path. He helps you let go of inner turmoil, release fear or depression, heals relationships, and provides you with spiritual understanding and insights. He is regarded as one of the wisest archangels, your personal psychologist who helps remove toxins from thoughts and emotions, releases stubborn anger and unforgiveness. If you are discouraged or unhappy with a relationship or career, ask

archangel Uriel to help you let go of your inner turmoil and release fears, especially if you are in a relationship that is volatile and full of disappointments.

He also oversees earth changes and weather conditions and helps those involved with natural disasters, such as earthquakes, tsunamis, fires and hurricanes.

Colour: Yellow
Crystal: Amber

ZADKIEL (Righteousness of God)
Zadkiel is the archangel of prayer and forgiveness of self and others, of mercy and tolerance. If you are full of bitterness, anger, hate, resentment towards self and others, he will help you transmute these negative emotions into love and light. Sometimes you may find it difficult to tolerate the behaviour of others. Ask for guidance to help you to soften your heart to love, to respect the situation or the person and to forgive yourself. He will help you see the other person's point of view as well as any negative aspect of self that you are unable to see, and find the positive in the situation.

In the angelic kingdom, he is considered to be the Angelic Ambassador of Benevolence, and his forte is to help discover the Divine aspect within you. He works with the high frequency spiritual energy of the Violet Flame of transmutation. He has the ability to see beyond our earth-based perceptions of our relationships, and promotes forgiveness of self and others to find peace and love on our shared paths. He also helps with memory functions to assist remembering important information.

Colour: Indigo blue
Crystal: Lapis Lazuli

Some of the other archangels that have crossed my path are:

ARIEL (Lion or Lioness of God)

Archangel Ariel is the angel in charge of all environmental issues, including the healing and protection of all wildlife both on land and in the sea. If you are a nature lover and need help protecting the environment, recruit archangel Ariel. He also helps manifest emergency money or other supplies needed for your day-to-day life to fulfil your life purpose.

AZRAEL (Whom God helps)

Although often referred to as the Angel of Death, he is not a frightening angel. He has a negative reputation owing to man's fear of death. When a soul is ready to cross over he comforts and helps the soul to depart the physical world and enter the spiritual world. He also comforts those who are left behind to grieve. If you are experiencing deep sadness which may be due to your deep desire to feel God's love, archangel Azrael will assist you to move through your sadness, find God's love that is within you and help you with your spiritual growth.

He also aids the clergy of all religions, spiritual teachers, hospice workers and grief counsellors. When someone has lost a dear one or there is a major disaster in the world, where human lives are lost, you can request archangel Azrael to shower love and support on those who are grieving.

HANIEL (Grace of God)
He carries all the lost secrets of natural healing abilities and of natural remedies. Being associated with moon energies, he teaches you to harness the moon's energy into natural healing potions, powders, lotions and crystals. He also helps understand astronomy and astrology.

He encourages beauty, grace, patience and gentleness. Archangel Haniel's gentle energies help bring grace and serenity for your first date, being interviewed for a job, or making an important presentation. He also helps with all feminine issues such as menopause, menstruation and so on.

JEREMIEL (Mercy of God)
If you have difficulty moving forward spiritually, he will help you review your life, make positive changes and guide you to the next steps on your path. He also assists in releasing fear and unforgiveness, bringing in mercy and clarity to any situation. He is the angel of prophetic visions and dream interpretations, who also inspires and motivates you to spiritual acts of service.

METATRON (One who serves behind the Throne)
Metatron is a fiery, energetic angel who has a special place in his heart for all children on this planet and in heaven. He helps children with their health, education, and teaches them to understand their spiritual awareness and power. He holds the blueprint of all creation and the sacred geometry patterns of the universe. His cube, written in ancient texts, is composed of all the sacred shapes of the universe. It is believed that he was Prophet Enoch, a mortal man who is now an archangel.

NATHANIEL (Fire of God)
He is continuously watching for your spiritual aspirations and uses the fire of God to burn away all old thoughts patterns beliefs and misconceptions that cause you to believe that you are separate from God. He helps you to find

clarity and guides you to fulfil your goals along your life path. He transforms and accelerates the shift of your consciousness from limited ego-self to your eternal self. He guides you to share your many lessons and gifts with others to bring happiness into your life.

RAGUEL (Friend of God)
He resolves arguments, mediates in disputes and encourages harmony in families and groups. He is the defender of the unfairly treated. His chief role in heaven is to oversee all the other archangels and angels to ensure they are working together in harmony according to Divine Order and Will.

If you need help in creating harmony and resolving conflicts in relationships, archangel Raguel will act as lawyer, jury and judge. If your life is full of arguments and disagreements with family members, especially at Christmas, Thanksgiving, Ramadan, Diwali, Chinese, Hindu or Buddhist New Year, invoke archangel Raguel to bring harmony and peace to these family celebrations.

RAZIEL (Secrets of God)
Archangel Raziel knows all the secrets of the universe and how it operates. As he is deeply involved in bringing you the knowledge of the mysteries of your spiritual path, he can help

you release restrictive beliefs relating to your life path or your self-destructive behaviour and to understand esoteric material, thus increasing your ability to see, hear, know and feel Divine guidance.

REMLIEL (Friend of God)
Helps you to understand that you are more than a physical being and guides you to face your unwanted feelings, to see the difference between illusion and truth, flesh and spirit. When you are ready to transform your life, he provides the best conditions for your spiritual growth and helps you to face the negative patterns that you have denied, freeing you from suffering and pain. He awakens you to love, gratitude and the wealth of wisdom which opens your heart to experience God's love and union with your "I am Presence" your eternal self.

SANDALPHON (Brother)
"Brother" is in reference to his twin Metatron. It is believed Sandalphon was Elijah, the Prophet who is now an archangel who carries human prayers to God. He overseas powers of strength, abundance, beauty and joy. He will guide you to find your emotional scars of fear, guilt, imbalances in your thought patterns and feelings, to release them to open the flow of God's power.

Archangel Sandalphon helps with song writing, singing and other aspects related to music. Music and movement helps break down negative emotions and raise your vibrations.

UZZIEL (Strength of God)
He brings the gift of power and faith into your life to accelerate your spiritual growth. Faith is an inner knowing found deep within your being and works in a realm beyond human reason and understanding. Faith is a powerful energy which is available to you to be used consciously and constantly, to connect with your "I am Presence" and union with God. Ask archangel Uzziel to teach you the attitudes of Love, Surrender and Gratitude, to transcend and connect with your inner knowing. Faith is a powerful energy found deep within you. It guides your thoughts, feelings and actions towards your desired goals. Faith opens your heart and fills you with love, light and inner peace.

ZACHARAEL (Remembrance of God)
He helps you to surrender and align your will to God's will. Deep surrender is to become aware of your negative beliefs your attachment to material things and to release them. Surrendering opens your mind to true wisdom and understanding that all your soul's desires are satisfied. As you surrender, Archangel Zacharael will help you to fulfil the needs of your soul and fill you with God's unconditional love and light.

6. GUARDIAN ANGELS

Your guardian angel or personal angel is assigned to you, to be with you from the time of your birth to the time of your death and thereafter. It is believed that when a new soul is about to incarnate, angels apply for the post of guardian angel to the new soul. The angel with the talents and abilities best suited to the new soul's life path is given the job of guardian angel. Your guardian angel would have been assigned to you, when, as a new soul, you were ready to incarnate, has been with you lifetime after lifetime and will never leave your side.

Your guardian angel knows you inside out better than your best friend does, loves you unconditionally, without judgement or criticism and gives you extra love, care and support, especially when you are at your lowest. As you can share all your deepest, darkest thoughts and feelings with your guardian angel, you can refer to this angel as your personal angel friend. Everyone has at least two guardian angels but sometimes more are assigned to one person depending on the nature of their mission on this planet. In Islam the guardian angels, are known as Hafazas.

Ways in which your guardian angel can help:

- If you feel alone, lonely or abandoned, and want to brighten your day with loving energies, visualise your guardian angel by your side, feel the loving hug, the warmth and the sense of peace and calm around you and you will never feel alone again.

- When you are worried, doubtful or fearful, picture yourself handing over all your cares to your guardian angel to be taken away and healed. Trust your angel to provide you with insights and guidance to deal with the worries, doubts and fears of the day.

- When you have a major decision to make and you don't know what is right for you, ask for guidance to make the right choice. The guidance given may not be what you expect, but trust it to be the best for you to bring you peace of mind.

- If you are about to travel, ask for the best possible route to take. If you get lost while travelling, instead of phoning your friend, call your guardian angel to direct you to your destination.

- Your guardian angel will help you with simple things. For example, you could ask your guardian angel to help you select your clothes and colours for the day, which grocery store to go for the things you need, and so on.

- If you have a physical illness, or an injury, or are facing major surgery, seek medical attention first and then ask your guardian angel to help you heal. You will also be provided with mental and emotional healing.

- If you lose something ask your guardian angel to find it for you. Remember that nothing is lost in the eyes of God.

- If you are applying for a job or struggling to write a letter, an email, or speak to someone, your guardian angel will provide you with the right words.

- If you are suffering from emotional wounds, or a relationship breakup, feeling betrayed and alone, turn to your guardian angel to guide you to see the situation from another perspective so that you can feel peace of mind instead of pain.

- If you are having a relationship issue with a friend, family member or a colleague, you can ask your guardian angel to speak to their guardian angel to help you both to resolve your relationship difficulty. The communication is always between the two guardian angels and not between you and the other person's guardian angel. Your guardian angels know the truth about you both, your pure innocent selves which neither of you may not be able to see;

therefore they are in a better position to help
you and show you how to resolve the situation
with love.

I am constantly in touch with my guardian angel.
When I first started calling on my guardian
angel, I felt I might be bothering her for every
little thing that I felt was not quite right in my
life. However, after having worked with her for a
while I now realise that the more I ask for help,
the more I receive.

7. EARTH ANGELS

Angels have never been incarnated nor have they left the side of God. For some unknown reason a few angels wanted to experience human emotions. In order to do this they split off fragments of themselves, which left the safety of the angelic realm and incarnated as humans on this planet. The soul of the earth angel is the fragment of the unconditional love of the angel that resides in the angelic realm and is connected to God.

Earth angels have a unique essence about them and in their purest form are intuitive, empathetic, sensitive and very giving. Earth angels push themselves to give their very best to others to the point of self-sacrifice and personal emotional turmoil. Without knowing why, they will be drawn to friendships and love relationships that need counselling and healing and will be attracted to professions such as nursing, counselling and teaching, or will have a very close and caring relationship with family and friends. They are always compelled to help others and be there for everyone else except themselves.

After a while, conflicting emotions start to surface and their life becomes a struggle. They will have the desire to change yet will feel guilty to put themselves first thus continuing to give again and again to the same people who have hurt them in the past. Not knowing how to say no, they will feel trapped in a vicious circle. They will start to experience deep sadness without being able to understand why. When they realise that this sadness and longing is the call of their soul to reconnect with God and their true being of unconditional love, they will say," Enough is enough," and turn within themselves to find the angelic qualities of love, compassion and inner wisdom and joy and bring them into their own lives and continue to help others to seek the same qualities resting within each soul.

8. WHAT ATTRACTS ANGELS?

When I started calling the angels for help, I spent quite some time trying to learn their names, qualities, colours and so on, and at times, when I was faced with a situation and I could not remember the specific angel's name, I used to get cross and frustrated with myself. This had to change, because instead of love and peace I was experiencing stress. I decided to write to my guardian angel for an answer to, "What attracts angels?" I realised that angels are attracted to the vibration of energy. All your thoughts and feelings whether negative or positive, broadcast a vibration of energy which the angels are attracted to.

When life becomes stressful and you are ready to make personal changes, you may not know where to begin, or be aware of the vast amount of help that is available to you from the angelic kingdom. When you make your desire for change through a heartfelt request, the angels will feel the energy vibrations of your request and will make their presence known to you. Their energies are warm, gentle and very subtle and you will be enveloped in overwhelming calmness and peace. A prayer or request for assistance does not need any words; just focus on your heart's deepest desire and the angels will respond.

Angels do not show themselves or interfere in your life's path. They are always by your side waiting quietly, lovingly and gently for you to call on them for help.

9. THE ALTAR

History states that in earlier times an altar was a temporary structure originally constructed outdoors and its primary function was as a place of sacrifice. It is believed that a human sacrifice or the killing of an animal on altars was an attempt to commune with God, to participate in Divine life. The applying of the blood symbolised the sacred life force. As man has evolved, the practice of human or animal sacrifice is no longer practised.

Nowadays an altar is a sacred space of protection from outside forces, where Divine energy is gathered and sent out to do what you want accomplished. In homes, altars now often function as a place to quieten the mind, body and spirit from modern day stresses and to commune with God. In places of worship, altars are used to hold Holy Scriptures, candles or flowers.

Before you set up an altar, clarify your intentions.

Why do you want an altar?
As a place to pray or meditate?
As a haven of peace and quiet?

To decide on the location, go with your inner guidance which will never let you down. The location can be a quiet corner of any room in your house, a corner of a table or desk, or a corner of a shelf. You can create your own sacred space anywhere, even within your body.

Before you set up your altar, clear the space by sprinkling salt water, burning incense, ringing bells or just intend that the space is cleared as you give the area a good dust and polish. Altars are often covered with fabric, and some religious traditions use particular colours or materials. Choose any colour that resonates with you. You can place on your altar any objects you like, such as images that are sacred to you, a cross, a statue or a picture of Jesus, Quan Yin, Buddha, Mohamed, any Hindu gods and goddesses or deities that you are familiar with, a copy of your prayer book, a religious script or your favourite poem or quote. You can also add fresh flowers or a small plant, a candle, an oil lamp and so on.

You can also place items to represent the four elements, angels, seasons and directions:

Element:	Fire
	Candle, oil lamp, or incense
Angel:	Archangel Michael
Season:	Autumn
Direction:	South

Element	Air
	A feather, a statue, picture of a bird
Angel:	Archangel Raphael
Season:	Spring
Direction:	East

Element	Water
	A bowl of water or Holy water
Angel:	Archangel Gabriel
Season:	Winter
Direction:	West

Element	Earth
	A crystal, fresh flowers, a plant or a small bag of sand
Angel:	Archangel Uriel
Season:	Summer
Direction:	North

Adorn your altar with objects that are personally symbolic to you. It can be something that someone special in your life has gifted to you or something that has a special connection to you. Before placing them on the altar, meditate on each item: its history, its purpose on the altar, and say a little prayer of gratitude. Use your altar to pray, meditate, daydream or to write in your journal.

It is also possible to create an altar to carry with you in a small bag. All you need are a few items such as pictures of any angels, gods or goddesses, a crystal, a small candle or special gifts from family or friends.

10. CRYSTALS

Everyone is attracted to diamonds, rubies, emeralds and sapphires, which are prized gemstones. From the dawn of history, crystals have been regarded as gifts from heaven in many parts of the world. The uniqueness of the crystals gives them the power to protect, strengthen, uplift and enhance the energy field around you. Crystals help you to gain access to the angelic realm.

The following list gives some of the crystals that may be used for angelic communication.

Amber is a resin. It is successful at lifting the heaviness of burdens, allowing happiness to come through, as well as helping to release toxins from the mind and body and find the soul within you.

Amethyst is a dark purple stone that is extremely powerful, with high spiritual vibrations, it quietens the mind develops intuition and removes negative thought patterns in order to receive messages from the Divine.

Angelite is the perfect stone for conscious contact with the angelic realm; its calming energy brings in faith and inner peace.

Apatite develops psychic gifts, deepens meditation and raises the 'kundalini,' it connects to a very high level of spiritual communication, opening the heart chakra as well as the ear chakra. It is a useful stone to have around hyperactive or autistic children.

Apophylite creates a conscious connection between the physical and the spiritual realms, it enhances clear sight and stimulates intuition and also helps you to look within and break down negative behaviour, which may have come from past lives.

Aquamarine helps to calm the nerves, gives clarity of mind and aids personal creativity. It assists in opening the sixth sense and in giving the ability to communicate with the higher realms.

Azurite eliminates illusion and provides links with creativity, inspiration and intuition.

Blue Calcite clears the chakras and helps recall messages from higher realms.

Celestite very gently attunes you to the angelic realm and brings in higher levels of consciousness.

Cherry Opal has a very fine vibration, this stone helps to activate clairvoyance and clairsentience, to help clear blocked Ajna chakra (third eye), and to bring out the love and passion within you.

Citrine heals old patterns and helps manifest the abundance of the universe.

Danburite is a highly spiritual stone; it activates both the intellect and higher consciousness linking them into the angelic realm.

Emerald is the stone of "unconditional love," which assists in acquiring deeper spiritual insight, introduces your "I am Presence," your connection to God and to the divinity within you. It inspires love, prosperity, kindness, tranquillity, balance, patience and the power to heal.

Fluorite calms the mind and induces greater concentration, helps to grasp and communicate with the higher and more abstract concepts of the inner self, and also balances the intuitive and intellectual aspects of the mind. Helps opening the Ajna chakra (third eye) developing spiritual awareness.

Herkimer Diamond stimulates clear knowing, clear seeing and telepathy. It clears and opens the chakras for spiritual energy to flow and brings the soul's purpose forward.

Galena brings balance and harmony between the physical and the spiritual planes.

Lolite is a stone of prophesy, it awakens and encourages intuition and guides you along your spiritual path.

Labradorite is a mystical and protective stone, brings in light raises consciousness and connection with the universal energies, and enhances psychic gifts.

Lapis Lazuli awakens the ability to see the non-physical world and higher dimensions, promotes clarity of vision and encourages purification.

Larimar is a spiritual stone that opens new dimensions and promotes angelic communication.

Malachite helps open the heart to love and enhances spiritual sight, it soothes and calms, helps foster patience and inner peace. This excellent stone balances the emotions and helps nurture visualisation.

Moonstone helps increase spiritual frequency, to connect with higher levels of the angelic realms.

Petalite is also known as the angel stone; this crystal opens higher consciousness, aids spiritual purification and helps with hearing the messages from the angels.

Quartz (Clear) draws blessings of the Divine and intensifies spiritual awareness and is an excellent stone for healing, meditation and spiritual development. It stimulates the Sahasrara chakra (crown) and activates higher consciousness.

Quartz (Aqua Aura) stimulates the throat chakra and aids communication from the higher realms. As well as being used to release negativity from the emotional, physical and mental bodies.

Quartz (Elestial) is an "enchanted crystal" that brings with it the concepts of Shiva, helps you to go deep within the self in order to find your soul self and to fulfil your mission on this planet.

Quartz (Phantom) symbolises universal awareness helps to access the Akashic records – to read past lives and recover repressed memories. It is a good stone to increase clairaudience.

Quartz (Singing) has a very powerful and high pitched "Om" vibration, combining the healing vibrations of Mother Earth and the energy of the stars. It also stimulates the ear chakras and helps correction of hearing deficiencies.

Rose Quartz is a stone of unconditional love and compassion; it opens and purifies the heart to receive the outpouring of Divine love that God and the angels transmit daily.

Ruby stimulates and balances the heart chakra.

Selenite is a translucent stone of comfort, peace, safety and protection, its high vibrations bring clarity of mind to access angelic communication.

Seraphinite is a stone of spiritual enlightenment and healing. It works on a subtle level.

Smithsonite assists accessing knowledge and healing from the higher astral planes during sleep/dreamtime and helps align emotions with the heart, allowing greater potential for personal growth and deeper relationship with self.

Sugilite represents spiritual love and wisdom; it opens all energy centres to inspire spiritual awareness.

Tanzanite allows for communication with the higher realms, facilitates visions and activates intuitive abilities.

Tourmaline releases fear and negative thought patterns and connects with your higher consciousness. It balances and calms the troubled mind and attracts inspiration.

Turquoise brings in emotional balance, peace of mind and creative expressions; it aids in developing intuition, brings in wisdom and is a reminder of your spiritual inheritance and beauty.

Watermelon Tourmaline a bi-coloured stone is the best available healer of the heart. The green treats the emotional wounds the heart has stored, while the pink inspires the flow of love. It also helps with clear communication with the higher realms.

Zoisite transforms negative energies into positive energy, assists in the awareness of the dormant abilities within the mind and stimulates your sixth sense.

11. FRAGRANCES

Fragrances are used by all religions and cultures in places of worship, at work or home. Every religion uses some sort of flower essence, resin or fresh flowers for purification and to connect with the Divine. In the Bible both in the Old and New testaments burning of incense are mentioned. It is a symbol of spiritual cleansing and it has been used in Christian worship since ancient times.

Muslims describe paradise as having the fragrance of musk, ginger, amber, rose and jasmine from the Garden of Eden. They also use rosewater in mosques and holy places. In the Jewish tradition, at the end of the Sabbath, a candle is burnt over a spice box containing cinnamon sticks, star anise, whole cloves, whole nutmeg, cardamom seeds and fennel.

Tibetans burn bundles of juniper near the roof of the house to open the sky door so that their prayers can be heard. Buddhists use a handful of incense sticks such as nag champa, camphor and juniper at the shrines before prayers. In Hinduism jasmine, sandalwood, rose, camphor, tuberose and lotus are some of the incenses used in shrines and homes. In the east people are more aware of their spiritual aspects and the air is full of the rich smell of flowers and the burning incense throughout the day. Every evening, to the fragrance of burning incense in the shrines and homes, is added the smell of cooking with aromatic herbs and spices.

In Native American culture, herbs such as sweet grass, cedar and sage are used in sweat lodges which are ceremonial saunas or sweat baths. A sweat bath is common to many ethnic cultures found in North and South America, Asia, Eastern and Western Europe, and Africa. They are used as a cure for illness, revitalisation of aching muscles, getting the body clean, for spiritual renewal, purification of the mind, body, spirit and reaching higher consciousness. During these ritual purification ceremonies, many higher beings have appeared to give guidance.

Burning fragrances is said to be a sign that you are ready to receive Divine guidance. Fragrances evoke emotions and memories of your divine connection to God. They purify your mind and keep you alert and ready to receive Divine guidance. All fragrances have their own frequency of vibrations and as angels are attracted through vibrations, fragrances bring the angels closer to you.

Amber - Encourages harmony, balance, inspiration and inner knowing.

Basil - Clears the ego mind that puts a barrier preventing contact with the angels. It assists in spiritual awakening and awareness.

Bay - Stops you dwelling on what has been and helps to create a positive note.

Black Pepper - Being very protective, helps to release fear of reuniting with the spiritual aspects of self.

Camphor - The fragrance of the warrior angels, cleanses, purifies and protects the soul, bringing freedom and enlightenment.

Cardamom - Stimulates the spiritual senses, awakens and clears the mind for insights on how to improve your spiritual practices.

Cinnamon - Invites love from the higher realms, transforming sorrow into happiness. Gives courage to step into the unknown.

Clove - Releases fear when in need of angelic assistance. It is also used to give thanks for angelic assistance.

Cypress - In times of bereavement, brings in angels to console those who are grieving.

Frankincense - Is woody, spicy and warming, helps achieve heightened spiritual awareness and to keep the heart in pure love and understanding.

Geranium - Sweet smelling like the rose brings the angels of peace and love closer, while helping understand disappointments, and provide comfort and assurance to see the opportunities for self growth within these disappointments.

Ginger - It helps to break out of spiritual apprehension which restricts the ability to be free to walk the spiritual path. The fragrance of the fearless, brings protection, courage and strength of the angels.

Jasmine - A gift from God, an aroma from the heavens, it opens your consciousness to the kingdom of the shining ones. It also helps to soften and open your heart to love, compassion and forgiveness.

Juniper - Offers a protective shield and clears obstructions, assists in purification and brings beings of love and light into your environment. Clears the mind for angels to speak to your heart and mind.

Lavender - It gently lifts sadness and despair that covers the spirit. Brings closer the angels of compassion.

Lemon - Vitalises and purifies the mind, body and soul, bringing clarity, calmness and happiness.

Lemongrass - Helps overcome ego, victimhood and issues that block spiritual understanding.

Lotus - Helps to raise consciousness on the path to enlightenment, symbolising purity and resurrection.

Myrrh - Brings understanding and compassion and helps with self-forgiveness.

Nutmeg - Awakens the conscious mind to the dreams of the angelic realm.

Pine - Invites the angels of love to help with humility, surrender and generosity.

Rose - Sweet, heavenly and intoxicating a fragrance of the angels which transports you to the ethereal realm, opens the heart and brings in the pure love of the Divine.

Sage - Brings the wisdom of the ages into the heart, clears and purifies the environment to bring in the energy of love and light.

Sandalwood - Sweet, warm and lingering a bridge between heaven and earth, releases negative energies, anger, resentment, fear and unforgiveness.

Spikenard - Contacts the angels of potentiality and reveals the secrets of the soul.

Stargazer Lily - Brings innocence and purity, along with the more modern connotations of honour and aspiration. The stargazer lily is known for the stunning appearance of its star shaped bloom and the distinctly sweet fragrance, a majestic masterpiece.

Tuberose - Brings about a transformation of character, dispelling negative attitudes and instilling positive resolve. The intoxicating fragrance of the tuberose is sweet, floral and honey like, with spicy and narcotic undertones.

12. MANDALA OR GRID

Creating grids is like creating mandalas. Mandala means "circle" in the classical Indian language of Sanskrit. A grid or mandala is a reminder of your relationship to the Divine world, which is within your body and mind and extends beyond into the universe. A grid brings in the energy of love and light of the angelic realms into the physical realm. It creates a sense of tranquillity and peace and draws your focus to the Divine. It's a reminder to focus on your divine self.

Beforehand it is good to have a clear idea as to why you want to create a grid and what its purpose is. A grid can be a place of meditation or a centre point for attracting Divine energy. The size can be large enough for you to sit in the middle, or place on your altar, a windowsill, under your bed, a corner of your office desk, in your car or outdoors. You can even make a small one to carry around with you. The size does not matter; whether big or small, it will have the same power.

An angelic grid can be in the shape of a circle or a triangle. A circle represents the celestial circle of the sun, the moon, the earth and the other planets. It also represents the conceptual circle of family, friends, community and the circle of life. For a circle grid you can use the crystals associated with the twelve zodiac signs, the seven chakra coloured stones or any of the crystals that have an affinity with the angels.

If you decide to use a triangular grid, it should be an equilateral triangle where all three sides are the same size. In Christianity the number three, represent God the Father, God the Son and God the Holy Spirit. In Hinduism three represents the Trimuti of Shiva, Brahma and Vishnu. The number three also represents the Mind, Body and Spirit.

Once you have a clear intention as to the purpose, size and location of the grid, you may wish to clear the space. This can be done with pure intention or any space-clearing method you are familiar with. For this grid you could place three clear quartz crystals on each side of the triangle and three rose quartz or angelite in the middle.

When choosing crystals follow your guidance. If you have not used them before, the easiest way to pick the right ones, is to stand or sit in front of a few crystals, close your eyes, take a few deep breaths and relax. Ask the crystals, "Which one of you wants to be on my grid?" Open your eyes and the first one you see is the right crystal. Do the same with the next one until you have all the crystals you need for the grid. Another way to choose a crystal is to pick one with your non-dominant hand and hold it for a couple of minutes, if it vibrates in your hand or any part of your body, then it is the right crystal for the grid. Once you bring the crystals home, or have selected them from your personal collection of crystals, give them a good wash and you can place them in the sunlight or moonlight for a couple of hours. If you are placing them in sunlight, avoid direct sunlight, as the sun's strong rays may fade their colours.

Once you have placed the crystals on the grid, sit quietly next to it, say a simple prayer of dedication for the crystals to act as a bridge between heaven and earth and to deepen your connection to receiving guidance from the angelic realm. Visualise lines of white light connecting each stone with the angelic realm, around you and your surroundings. Thank the angelic beings for coming into your life, for their love, support and guidance. The grid is now activated and will continuously bring in love and light.

A grid changes the energy around its vicinity and expands the energy fields within the environment. It helps open your mind and body to love, to make choices without guilt regarding what is right for you. It moves old cellular thought patterns that may have created a negative field of energy within and around your body. Some of these cellular patterns may have been inherited through an age-old hereditary pattern from some far off ancestor or through the beliefs and thought patterns of your society, friends and family. If you have any issues weighing on your mind, sit near the grid, focus on your breath, quieten your mind, and write down the question or issue that is unsettling you. Surrender to the angels any distracting thoughts or worries that may arise. Pay close attention to any ideas, visions, colours, words or feelings that come to you. When you are close to a grid, you will feel a stronger communication with your angels. You may also hear celestial music or soft whirring sounds. These are some of the signs that you may experience near a grid. Once again thank the angels for their love and support.

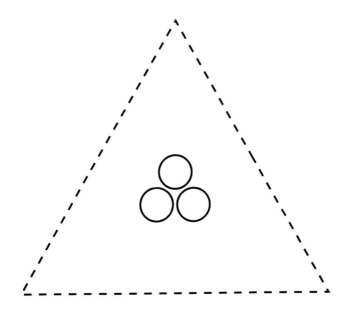

Fig. 1 Triangular angelic grid.

13. COMMUNICATING WITH YOUR ANGELS

There is nothing special to know or learn about communicating with your angels. You do not have to go into a meditative state or raise your vibrations. It is like talking to your friends; you are totally relaxed yet excited to be in their company. You often trust your friends with your secrets and ask them for guidance and advice on various situations that may arise in your life. It is exactly the same when you communicate with your angels, except that you may or may not share all your innermost or "darkest secrets" with your friends for fear that they may betray your trust, but your angels will never betray your trust and confidentiality.

Angels are always by your side ready to help you; nothing is too small or too big for them. There are unimaginable numbers of angels waiting to help you. Do not worry that you will wear them out if you keep asking them for guidance every minute of the day. It's the opposite because angels know that you are on this planet to grow spiritually to learn compassion, and unconditional love. They are here to help you to release all illusions and obsessions you may have created such as greed for money, security, status, accumulation of material things and so on. As their primary function is to guide you to follow your heart, the more you call on them the happier they are to help. When you do this, you will also be helping the angels to fulfil their function as messengers of God's pure love and light.

There are several ways in which you can communicate with your angels. They are as follows -

WRITE

If a situation or someone has triggered any anger, fear, frustration, jealousy, resentment or unforgiveness within you, share your innermost feelings with the angels and ask them for guidance to help you understand the emotion and release it. As you write to your angels, you will feel a sense of calm and you will be able to see the positive aspects of the situation.

Writing is a useful tool for conscious connection to higher guidance. Make a list of your questions, write them in your journal, leaving some space between each question, relax and wait for the answers. They may come instantaneously or they may pop into your head later. It is best to write down whatever guidance that comes to you. Even if it does not make sense, do not try to analyse the message while you are recording it. When you read it back later, it will make sense and you will be able to put into action the guidance received.

Writing to the angels is sometimes referred to as automatic writing, where you hold a pen loosely in your dominant hand and it moves across the page of its own accord or you write down positive thoughts that go through your mind. The messages you receive are from God and the angelic realm. This is not to be confused with writing with your non-dominant hand, where the answers come from your subconscious mind.

MEDITATE

Meditation is simply the quietening of the mind and body, an opportunity for you to get to know your angels. Find a quiet space where you will not be disturbed for thirty minutes or so. Take a few deep breaths; relax, let go, quieten your mind and body. Focus on your question and direct the question to the angels and stay in that quiet state until you have received clarity. Always make a record of the guidance you receive.

DREAM

Invite your angels into your dream state to give you advice. If you have a question, direct it to them as you fall asleep. Keep a dream journal and on waking record your dreams even if they do not make sense. After a few days of recording your dreams you will see a pattern emerging which will give you a clearer answer to your question.

TALK

If you are unable to find time to write or meditate, you can always hold a mental conversation with your angels. You can talk to your angels while you are having a shower, sitting in a traffic jam, or when doing your daily chores. Talking to the angels is like talking to your friend on the phone or face-to-face.

CALL

When you are facing a stressful or traumatic situation and you are agitated and not able to focus, you may phone a friend for help. The next time you are in a similar situation, take two or three deep breaths and say, "Angels please help me. I don't know how to deal with this situation." As angels know all your needs and wants, they will guide you and give you a solution. Their guidance may come as a thought, someone may say something, or the words of a song that is helpful and you start to feel a sense of calm and are able to deal with it. This is God's way of sending you help.

Do not be afraid to ask your angels for anything and everything you need. To communicate with your angels, release all your fears, be totally relaxed. When you feel an overwhelming sense of calm your attention is drawn to a more natural direction of love and trust, and you become aware of the angels answers. The more you relax and release all your fears and expectations; you will be able to communicate with the angels.

14. DEVELOPING YOUR INTUITIVE SKILLS

You do not have to be a psychic or have any special powers to experience the presence of the angels. Psychics sometimes unknowingly receive messages from the astral plane where ego-based spirits dwell, who may and can interfere with the messages received.

Angels are from God's plane of pure love and light and communicate via your inner knowing, the sixth sense. You do not have to search for the angels, or connect to them to receive guidance. Angels know all your desires and innermost thoughts and feelings and are constantly communicating with you, yet they will not intervene until you call them for help. They are always by your side waiting for you to become aware of their presence and your call for assistance.

There is nothing to learn about communicating with your angels. We are all born with six senses not five. You can lose the five senses of touch, taste, hearing, sight and smell, but the sixth sense is one that you cannot lose because it is your connection to the Divine. Ego-based fears may have made you doubt or shut down your sixth sense through which the angelic kingdom communicates with you.

Very often you dismiss the guidance of the angels by referring to their help as coincidences or chance events, but they are carefully planned by God and orchestrated by the angels. Have you noticed when you thought of a friend and within a day or two you heard from him or her? Have you misplaced a letter, keys, wallet or cell phone and asked yourself "Now where did I leave my……….?" when suddenly a hunch guides you to a place where you find the lost item. When the phone rang and before you answered it, you knew who was at the other end. This is an angel crossing your path and giving you messages. You may also have experienced certain situations in your life where you had a suspicion that God had intervened and given you strength and courage. God and the angels are in constant communication with you. All you have to do is be consciously aware of the various forms in which Divine communication is transmitted.

Angels respond to your heartfelt request for assistance. When you are facing a stressful or traumatic time in your life, the last thing on your mind is to go into a meditative state to seek the assistance of the angels. Instead, recall that extra angels are by your side to support you with love. Turn to God and the angels with your heartfelt request. It can be as simple as "Angels please help me as I do not know how to deal with this situation," and you will receive immediate clarity.

As each person is unique, angels show themselves in different ways. Some see them in their mind's eye, some feel their presence, others may hear the angels via their non-physical ears and there are others who just know when angels are around. If you see orbs, flashes of coloured or white light, or feel sudden warmth or a gentle touch, you know that your angels are around you. They may even make their presence known through words in a song, a chance conversation you hear on the street, a sequence of numbers such as 444, 111, 338, 545, by dropping a feather where there are no birds, or by a beautiful fragrance around you that cannot be identified or described. Seeing triple numbers is a sign that Divine force is assuring you that are not alone.

In order to receive messages from your angels it is good to be aware of your sixth sense and of the four ways through which you can receive angelic communication.

CLEAR FEELING
The majority of people have a clear feeling of the angels. They sense things that are physically intangible. Clear feeling is an inner feeling, a 'vibe,' 'a gut feeling.' It is always good to honour your physical sensations and emotional feelings. Learn to become aware of the part of your body that is affected when you are frustrated, sad or angry. Write it down in your journal.

When you feel joy, again notice where in your body you feel the energy of joy and record it. Next call on the angels and become aware of the difference between your own feelings and theirs. You will feel theirs as a gentle, calming and loving energy.

To increase the awareness of your clear feeling to receive messages from the angels, gather a few household items such as salt, rice, flour, pepper, milk, water, silk, cotton, things from your garden, flowers, leaves, or stones. Spend some time getting to know these items. Close your eyes, pick one item at a time in your hands and feel it, smell it, look at it through your mind's eye, taste it, listen to it. Using all six senses to get to know the feelings they create in your hands and your body. Note them in your journal. As you practise, you will learn to differentiate between your physical sensations and those of the angels. Your awareness of their presence will also increase.

The chakra, crystals and angels associated with clear feeling are:-

Chakra: Anahata (Heart) and Manipura
            (Solar Plexus)
Crystals: Rose quartz, Citrine, Aquamarine,
            Yellow tiger's eye
Angels: Angels of Clairsentience
            Archangel Raguel

CLEAR SEEING

The next group of people have the ability to see things very clearly. They have a photographic or visual memory, they may also be light-sensitive. Clear seeing is when messages are received as charades, colours, shapes, pictures or images in your mind's eye or beyond your mind. You may also see auras, the energy field around a physical body and apparitions. Sometimes you may receive messages via your dreams. It is a good practice to keep a dream journal because sometimes a dream may be puzzling but if you have written it down, as you receive insights and realisations during next few days, it will start to gain significance.

To increase the ability of clear seeing set out a few simple items in front of you, for example, a plant, a flower, a crystal, a lighted candle, a picture, a statue and so on. Look at each item one at a time for a few minutes with your physical eyes. Close your eyes and move this image into your mind's eye, holding it there open your eyes and describe everything you saw. Write this down in your journal. With a little practice and awareness, you may start to see with your mind's eye, even when your physical eyes are open.

Sometimes the message you receive may be symbolic, and difficult to understand. For example you could see a green light, this could mean you need healing or "proceed" with your goals. In these instances, do not give your own interpretation. Always ask the angels to explain the symbolic messages to you in a simple manner in which you could understand them.

The chakra, crystals and angels associated with clear seeing are:-

Chakra: Ajna (Third Eye)
Crystal: Lapis Lazuli, Amethyst, Blue calcite
Angels: Angels of Clairvoyance
             Archangel Michael,
             Archangel Raphael,
             Archangel Haniel,
             Archangel Raziel

CLEAR HEARING

Clear hearing is the ability to hear things that are inaudible to the physical sense of hearing. Clear hearing comes via your ear chakras, which are located above the left and right eye at a 30 degree angle inside your head.

Have you ever heard your name called when no one was around?
Have you heard beautiful celestial sounding music?
Have you repeatedly heard a song in your head or on the radio?

In this way your angels are trying to get your attention to their presence.

To clear your ear chakras, each morning, before getting out of bed, do as follows:-

Close your eyes
Breathe deeply
Make your intention clear that you wish to hear the angels
Ask the angels a question and wait
Relax and Listen

Always pay close attention to everything you hear in your mind, your ear chakras and your physical ears, because sometimes the voice may be very faint yet gentle and focused. With a little practice you will be able to distinguish between the voice of your ego and that of the higher realms.

The chakra, crystals and angels associated with clear hearing are:-

Chakra: Ear (non physical)
Crystal: Rutilated quartz, Pink tourmaline, Singing quartz, Phantom quartz, Petalite
Angels: Angels of Clairaudience
            Archangel Zadkiel

CLEAR KNOWING

The messages are mini transmissions that pop into your mind. They come as repetitive messages. A clear knowing person is aware of things, and may be able to answer questions with facts and figures, not understanding why others can't. If you ask them, "How did you know that?" they will look surprised and say, "It just came into my head." This group is referred to as claircognisants.

Clair cognisance comes from the 17th century French, clair (clear) and connoissance (knowledge). It is a form of extra sensory perception, where the person has the ability to know something without a physical explanation how or why they know it. Those who are claircognisant are very mentally oriented, analytical, and good at understanding abstract concepts and problems. To increase claircognisance, keep a journal and note down messages received during dreamtime or during the day. Spending quiet time with nature also helps with clear knowing.

The chakra, crystal and angels associated with clear knowing are-

Chakra:	Sarasrara (Crown)
Crystal:	Clear Quartz, Amethyst, Selenite, Herkimer diamond
Angels:	Angels of Claircognisance Archangel Uriel, Archangel Raziel

15. BLOCKS TO RECEIVING MESSAGES

Every human being is connected to God via their sixth sense. God and the angels are in constant communication daily with each and every person through their sixth sense. Yet there are many who think they are unable to receive communications from God and the angels because they do not have any special powers or psychic abilities.

If you believe you are unable to receive messages, this is because your ego-self has blocked your sixth sense, your natural ability to receive guidance from the higher realms. The ego-self through fear creates doubts in your mind such as -

Am I good enough to experience the presence of the angels?
What if I don't see the angels?
Is it true guidance?
Is it my imagination?

You can also block communication by straining too hard to see or hear the angels, by having expectations of how the answers should be delivered to you or by not asking for guidance. You may also be intimidated and a little frightened of what you may hear or not hear. Lack of trust and faith also creates blocks to receiving angelic messages.

If you are unable to sense the presence of the angels, it is possible that you may have blocked your sixth sense due to childhood incidents. For example, as a child you may have seen angels or fairies but adults told you otherwise and you shut yourself off from seeing them again. You may have blocked or shut down your Ajna chakra (third eye) due to your religious upbringing. Your primary ability is to feel the presence of the angels but your desire is to see or hear them, thus missing the angelic communication. It may also be due to some past life trauma. Whatever the reason, the root cause of the block is ego based fear with the result your mind is clogged with judgement, criticism and unforgiveness towards self and others, low self-esteem, self worth and lack of self confidence.

There is no right or wrong way to ask for God's guidance via the angels. It is your divine birthright to sense the presence of the angels and to receive their messages. Release all your fears, become aware and tune into the unique ability of your sixth sense. Ask the angels to help you release any limiting thoughts patterns and beliefs that prevent you from receiving messages from God via the angels. Trust and have faith in yourself that you can feel, see and hear the angels, and they will propel and support you every step of the way to follow your inner guidance.

16. TRUE GUIDANCE vs FALSE GUIDANCE

True guidance comes from God and the angels, it is accurate and reliable. False guidance comes from your ego-self, sometimes referred to as your lower self or shadow self. Your ego-self contains all your fears and illusions of self, the beliefs of society of how life should be and thus separated you from God's love and His true guidance which He transmits to you daily.

Awareness is important in discerning true guidance from false guidance. For example, while you are driving suddenly the thought comes into your mind, "Turn left on this road now" is true guidance but if your response is "what a silly thought, that road is out of my way," this is your ego giving you false guidance. You may get the urge to spend some time in nature one morning but if you ignore it and decide to do so the next day, you have ignored true guidance. True guidance will never lead you astray, nor will it cause pain or suffering to you or to others. True guidance is always in the moment of now, not in the future. False guidance often tells you to look to the future and fosters delay tactics which are caused by your own fears.

True guidance has a mature tone and is constant and repeats the same message over and over again until you take notice. It has a loving, warm and energising feel to it. It assures you of your success and empowers you by coming directly to the point. It sounds familiar and feels like a warm hug. True guidance talks about your life's purpose and how to be yourself, letting you know that you are equal and one with others. False guidance drains your energy, enthusiasm, and destroys your confidence, trying to tell you that you are better or worse than others and talks you into competing with others. It is confrontational and the messages are random and ever changing.

False guidance is ill conceived and hollow, keeps you thinking about the worst case scenarios, it's abusive and discouraging. False guidance says "don't even try" and will talk you out of true guidance. True guidance comes suddenly and completely. It feels natural and comforting and is consistent and encouraging. It says have trust and faith.

Sometimes by following false guidance and making miss-takes (not a spelling error) you learn to trust, have faith, listen and follow your true guidance.

17. EXPERIENCE THE ENERGIES OF THE ANGELS

ENERGIES OF THE ARCHANGELS

To feel the different energies of the angels around you, first find some quiet time where you will not be disturbed. Take a few deep breaths and relax. Call Archangel Michael, for example, to let you know how you can be aware of his presence. Notice any subtle changes in your body, surroundings, sounds that you may hear or visions that you may see. Make a note of them in your journal. Do not be discouraged if on your first attempt you are unable to experience the presence of the angel. This may be because you are not totally relaxed, or have expectations of how you should experience the energies of Archangel Michael. Your experience of Archangel Michael will be unique to you. Relax and let go of whatever that is restricting you from this wonderful experience. Write down in your journal your experiences. Once you are familiar with the energies of Archangel Michael, the next time you experience the same sensations you will know without going into a meditative state that he is around you. Follow the same procedure to familiarise yourself with the energies each of the other archangels and angels. After a while, you will be able to recognise the different energies of each of the archangels and the angels.

TO MEET YOUR GUARDIAN ANGEL

To feel the presence of your guardian angel, find a quiet place where you will not be disturbed for a few minutes. Take a few deep breaths and relax. Make clear your intention that you want to feel the presence of your guardian angel. Ask the angel to come forward and reveal to you the unique way of contact with you. Relax and be aware of any slight changes in your body; it may be a gentle tap on your shoulder, a tingling sensation on your cheek or on any part of your body, sudden warmth around you, or as if someone is sitting next to you. You may see a flash of white light or even hear a soft and gentle voice calling your name.

Do not be disappointed if on your first attempt you do not experience anything. It may be because you are not relaxed or on the other hand trying too hard. You may also have expectations of how your guardian should communicate with you. Keep trying and as you relax and let go of your expectations of how you would like your guardian angel to communicate with you, you will definitely be able to feel the presence of your guardian angel.

The presence of your guardian angel is always very subtle, calming, gentle and peaceful.

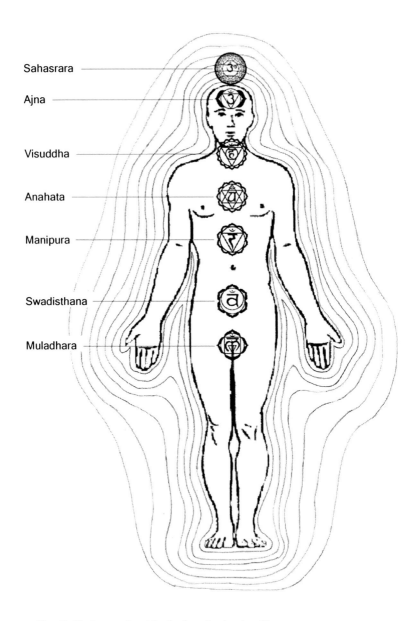

Sahasrara

Ajna

Visuddha

Anahata

Manipura

Swadisthana

Muladhara

Fig. 2 Chakra and subtle body ref. chapter 18.

72

18. CHAKRAS

Chakra means a wheel in the ancient Indian language of Sanskrit. Chakras are spinning wheels of energy, the opening for life force to flow in and out of your body. There are seven major chakras aligned along the spine, neck and skull, and many minor chakras located in the body. The seven major chakras connect your physical, mental and emotional bodies and bring about the development of a higher consciousness. Dysfunction in the chakras affects the flow of energy into and through each corresponding body part and subtle bodies. The subtle body is around the physical body and is referred to as a person's aura. It has seven layers corresponding to the seven major chakras.

Chakras are invisible to the human eye but can be perceived intuitively and look similar to funnels with petal-like openings.

The seven major chakras are:

Muladhara, the root chakra, is located at the base of the spine below the sacrum bone. It is the slowest spinning chakra. It represents the element earth, and is related to survival issues of money, career, material things, home, security and self-preservation. Worries related to these issues clouds the true nature of this chakra, which is innocence and causes an imbalance. Innocence is the quality by which you experience pure, childlike joy, and inner wisdom that is ever present in you, without the limitations of prejudice or conditioning. It gives you dignity, balance, and a tremendous sense of direction and purpose in life.

The angels, fragrances and crystals associated with this chakra are -

Colour	Red
Angel	Archangel Gabriel
	Archangel Sandalphon
Fragrance	Geranium
	Patchouli
	Sandalwood
	Rosewood
Crystal	Hematite
	Garnet
	Obsidian
	Tourmaline

Swadisthana, the sacral chakra, is located in the lower back, midway between your navel and the base of your spine and is related to the element of water, emotions and sexuality. It is the seat of pure creativity, and pure knowledge, the centre of attention and power of concentration. It is the source of inner inspiration and procreation, connecting you to others through thoughts, feelings, desires, cravings and sensations. When this chakra is out of balance, you may experience tiredness and lack of sleep or become addicted to food, drugs, cigarettes, alcohol and other substances.

The angels, fragrances and crystals associated with this chakra are -

Colour	Orange
Angel	Archangel Gabriel
	Archangel Chamuel
Fragrance	Jasmine
	Sandalwood
	Clary sage
	Lavender
Crystal	Carnelian
	Tiger's eye
	Amber

Manipura, the solar plexus chakra, is located two fingers below the centre of the ribcage on the spine and is related to the element of fire. Surrounding this chakra is the void, which represents spiritual mastery. In some spiritual traditions, this area is referred to as the "ocean of illusions" that needs to be crossed to attain enlightenment. When there is an imbalance it is dominated by fears, worries, stress and attachments of the ego-self. A healthy balanced Manipura brings energy, spontaneity and non-dominating power, the spiritual power of faith, trust and calmness so that you become Master of your life.

The angels, fragrances and crystals associated with this chakra are -

Colour	Yellow
Angel	Archangel Uriel
Fragrance	Frankincense
	Camomile
	Eucalyptus
	Rose
Crystal	Citrine
	Pyrite

Anahata, the heart chakra, is located in the centre of the spine. This chakra relates to love and relationships with family, friends and the Divine. It is the seat of love and joy, the gateway to the soul where your spirit, your true self resides. It promotes forgiveness and deep love and compassion to self and others, to have a sense of peace and calm and centeredness. It is from this centre that compassion and love are manifested.

The angels, fragrances and crystals associated with this chakra are -

Colour	Green or Pink
Angel	Archangel Chamuel
	Archangel Raphael

Fragrance	Rose
	Geranium
	Ylang ylang
Crystal	Rose quartz
	Ruby
	Emerald
	Bloodstone
	Malachite

Visuddha, the throat chakra, is located in the centre of the throat near the Adam's apple. It is related to thoughts and feelings of communication and creativity, representing the intellectual body, the ability of a person to express him or herself. This chakra is the seat of diplomacy, exhibiting the powers of understanding, detachment and clarity. Balancing this chakra removes all guilt and remorse, feelings of jealousy, tendencies to dominate others or feel dominated by others, transcending fear and promoting personal integrity and a kind and compassionate voice. This chakra is your connection with the "whole" and enables you to feel your oneness with God.

The angels, fragrances and crystals associated with this chakra are -

Colour	Blue
Angel	Archangel Michael
Fragrance	Rose
	Jasmine
	Sandalwood

	Frankincense
	Eucalyptus
Crystal	Turquoise
	Aquamarine
	Blue agate
	Lapis lazuli

Ajna, the brow chakra, is located on the forehead between the eyebrows. It is related to the act of seeing, both physically and intuitively. This chakra dissolves all your ego conditionings, habits and illusions. It is the gateway for your consciousness to ascend to the seventh chakra and beyond, the eye of wisdom, the seat of Divine intelligence where consciousness and unconsciousness merge and where the ability to create physical realities from mental realities happens instantaneously.

The angels, fragrances and crystals associated with this chakra are -

Colour	Indigo blue
Angel	Archangel Raphael
	Archangel Jophiel
Fragrance	Juniper
	Jasmine
	Sandalwood
	Frankincense
	Rose
Crystal	Amethyst
	Blue sodalite

Azurite
Iolite

Sahasrara, the crown chakra, integrates all the chakras with their respective qualities and is located on the top of the head. It is the seat of consciousness and pure awareness and is your connection to the Divine, a place of all knowledge, wisdom, understanding, spiritual connection and bliss. It represents the highest level of spiritual perfection and is the merging point of the personal energy field with the universal field. When open, a person experiences connection with the Divine and All That Is, I am That I am which signifies the purpose and meaning of life.

The angels, fragrances and crystals associated with this chakra are -

Colour	White or Gold
Angel	Archangel Zadkiel
	Archangel Michael
Fragrance	Frankincense
	Rose
	Jasmine
	Sandalwood
	Rosewood
Crystal	Clear quartz
	Selenite
	Diamond
	Herkimer diamond

19. CHAKRA CLEARING

Picture your chakra system like a railway network, where the main lines connect the main stations and from them many minor tracks lead to smaller stations. If there is a hold up at any of the main stations or on one of the main tracks, there will be delays that may even cause the network system to collapse. Similarly with your chakra system. If your energy flow is compromised by any of the major chakras, the flow of the energy of love and light into the rest of your chakra system and your body will be restricted. What clogs up the chakras are your thoughts and emotions. To keep the flow of energy clear and smooth, daily chakra clearing is essential, once in the morning and once in the evening. There are many different ways to clear your chakras; you may use one of the following or any other form of chakra clearing that you are familiar with.

WHITE LIGHT
Visualise a beam of white light coming from God source into your Sahasrara (crown) chakra, let the light penetrate any darkness or dimness from it. Next watch it move to your ear chakras, cleaning and clearing, moving to your Ajna (third eye) and then down the other major chakras. As the white light clears each chakra, see them shining brightly.

CRYSTALS

Using crystals are a powerful way to clear your chakras. Select the appropriate crystals for each, lie down and place them on top of your body on the locations of the chakras. Breathe deeply and tune into the vibrations of the crystals as they loosen and clear any toxic energies that may have accumulated in your chakras from your negative thoughts and emotions. Leave the crystals for at least fifteen minutes on your body.

GOLDEN BALL

Find a space where you will not be disturbed; sit quietly, take a few deep breaths and relax. Visualise a golden ball hovering over your head, pull it down through your Sahasrara (crown) chakra to your Muladhara (root) chakra; as it reaches the Muladhara, see it turn red, spinning and clearing the chakra. When you see the chakra shining ruby red, move your focus and the golden ball to your Swadisthana (sacral) chakra. It now turns orange, spinning and clearing the chakra until it is clean and shining brightly. As you move your attention to the Manipura (solar plexus) the ball turns yellow, spins and clears all toxic energies; the Manipura (solar plexus) shines a bright sunflower yellow. Continue moving up all the chakras. When the chakras are cleared, watch the golden ball shoot out of your Sahasrara (crown) chakra into the universe, taking all the toxic energies to be healed and turned into love.

ANGELS
Call on the angels to pour buckets of rainbow-coloured liquid through your Sahasrara (crown) chakra and clear your chakras and every cell in your body of all toxins.

CLEARING CHAKRAS WITH ARCHANGEL METATRON'S CUBE
Chakras can also be cleared using archangel Metatron's cube. Archangel Metatron is the angel who works with your highest potential. The use of his cube not only clears your physical chakras but your higher chakras as well. This cube is both three and multi-dimensional in nature, holding all the geometric shapes of the universe and representing perfection and wholeness.

You do not have to study or memorise the exact shapes in the cube. Just close your eyes, relax and ask Archangel Metatron to come with his cube and cleanse, heal and balance your chakras. Visualise the cube coming in through your crown chakra and let it spin. You may see it change shape or direction. As your chakras clear and shine, you will feel whole and complete and aligned with the blueprint for your life on this planet. Spend a moment to thank archangel Metatron for this wonderful gift.

During the day, if you experience stress, you can do a short chakra balance to release stress and energise yourself. To clear your chakras you could also use fragrances, sounds or affirmations with mudras. A mudra is a gesture or position usually curling, stretching and crossing the fingers and hands. This locks and guides the energy flow and reflexes to the brain.

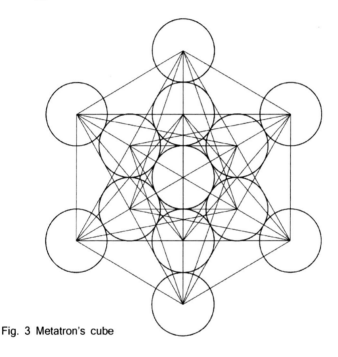

Fig. 3 Metatron's cube

THE VIOLET FLAME

The Violet Flame, sometimes referred to as the Violet fire, brings with it the qualities of mercy, forgiveness, freedom and transmutation. It has a unique energy that can heal physical, emotional and mental issues and it is believed to have been used by spiritual alchemists of the past to erase or transmute the cause, effect and memory of past mistakes.

The Violet Flame is invoked through a "decree" similar to a mantra. The simplest decree for the Violet Flame is, "I am a being of the Violet Flame, I AM the purity God desires." Start with just a few minutes every evening to help you to transmute whatever may have caused you stress during the day. Close your eyes, take a few slow deep breaths and go within your heart. Invoke the Violet Flame by repeating the decree three or nine times and gradually increase the repetitions. Visualise the Violet Flame in front of you, pulsating in endless shades of purple and pink. As you see yourself stepping into the middle of the Flame, focus on the issue or feeling that you wish to be transmuted by it. See the Flame curling up from beneath your feet, passing through and around your body and over your head.

Once you have finished decreeing you can say something like, " I ask that this Violet Flame be multiplied and used to assist all souls on this planet who are in need. Thank you."

Even a few minutes of the Violet Flame will produce results, but persistence is needed to change age-old habits.

20. ANGELIC GIFTS

It is God's will that you do not suffer or struggle in life. He does not want you to be judgemental or critical of yourself or others or to be cruel to each other, to plants or animals. Judgement, criticism and cruelty come from your negative thought patterns or ego-self, your illusionary self, which leads you to move away from the Divine and your life path.

Angels are your greatest teachers; they know your past, present and future. They also know your life purpose even if you are not aware of it. When you get distracted from your life path, as teachers they create situations and experiences in your life to get your attention and help you see the higher picture and bring your focus back to your life path.

They also give:

LOVE
Angels are always showering you with God's unconditional love. Love is self expression. Doing what you love in the moment and following your passion. Angels help you to see the difference between love from the outside - which is a job, husband, wife, partner, children, or approval, validation, security, appreciation, assurances, permission or direction from others which brings

us pain. Pain makes you forget that self love and self joy are all within. Self love is to love yourself unconditionally. When you find self love, you will see divine love within you and each and every human being. Love is being aligned with God and expressing your divinity of love, wisdom, compassion and joy to self and others.

AWARENESS

Awareness is differentiating between illusions and truth. Self awareness is seeing the false part of yourself, the negative attitudes such as judgement, and criticism of self and others. Awareness comes when you observe and understand yourself with no judgement, criticism or interference. Unawareness is when you live a life, where your thoughts, emotions, actions and reactions are all mechanical and these are generally someone else's patterns. At times, you may become aware that you are at a crossroad where you may have to choose between old ways of living and the desires of your soul. Awareness helps you to make the right choice and guides you to receive insights and realisations that will change you. The true part of your soul emerges and you will be filled with love, light, truth, wisdom and happiness.

PROTECTION

God and the angels always protect you. Therefore, you may ask, "Why do I need to ask for protection?" You may want to protect yourself if you are going to be in a situation where there may be a lot of fear and/or anger, or in an environment filled with negativity, protecting yourself will keep your vibrations high and stop you from picking up the negative energies of fear or anger from others. If someone or something has upset you, having protection around you keeps others safe from the energies of your negative thoughts and feelings. You can ask the angels to protect you from your negative thought patterns and actions that may be a stumbling block to the fulfilment of your Divine destiny. They also provide you with physical protection.

If you are worried about your physical safety, or the safety of a loved one, or as a parent you constantly worry about the safety of your children, placing protection around you and your loved ones stops you worrying about them and gives you peace of mind.

Asking for protection takes only a few seconds. As a daily routine, when you wake up in the morning, you can ask for personal protection; for your loved ones, your home, your car, your neighbourhood with a simple request: "Angels please protect me and……………. today." If you are in a life threatening situation and in an agitated or fearful state, all you need to say is "Angels, please protect me" and it is done. Keep repeating it like a mantra until you start feeling composed and you will be able to deal with the situation from a position of calmness, strength and clarity.

HEALING

Angels are the link to God's healing powers. When you suppress your emotions, stress and worries increase and they appear as physical illnesses. These are messages from your soul to tell you that you are moving away from your spiritual path. Angels are your greatest support system. They support you during the darkest times and the best times of your life. During times of despair, very often family and friends may not understand what you are going through or they may be too busy to listen to you. Angels have all the time in the world to listen, support and love you unconditionally. If you are experiencing unwanted emotional turmoil and your mind is full of negative mental clutter, ask the angels of change to help you focus on the angelic help available. Be open to receive the healing and see the positive side of the situation, thus helping you move forward.

CHANGE

If your mind is tortured by thoughts of fear, anger, resentment, guilt or jealousy and your life is full of stress, it is a call from your soul that something needs to be changed. Blaming others for your unhappiness, and trying to change them, is not going to make your life any better or bring you happiness. If you want a better life for yourself you need to take responsibility for your life, commit to change, and convert your negative thoughts and feelings into positive ones. As you do so, you will find that the behaviour of others, or what they think or say about you, will not bother you anymore. If you are facing unexpected or unwanted situations, or are unaware or afraid of the need to change, tune into your thoughts and emotions, so you can be willing to change. The angels will reach out, take your hand and show you the next steps in this process.

FORGIVENESS

Your soul wants to open your heart to forgiveness and love. Holding on to anger, hatred, jealousy, guilt, resentment or revenge, a need for control and insistence that the other person agrees with you will all make you feel self righteous and will keep you a prisoner of the situation and of life. Negative thoughts and emotions all cause you pain and suffering that builds up and results in health issues. If you hold on to your conviction that you are right and justified, in any area of your life, this will not bring a reconciliation or solution to the situation. Unforgiveness closes your heart and keeps you a prisoner of your illusions. Forgiveness starts when you stop criticising or judging yourself and others. Forgiveness is not saying, "You are right and I am wrong." To forgive, you don't even have to like the person. Forgiveness starts with the self. Forgiveness happens within you from the love that resides in your soul. Forgiveness simply requires changing your way of thinking about the situation or person and your behaviour, and so freeing your mind. Forgiveness is a great healer. When you forgive you feel more at peace with yourself. Forgiveness is a gift to yourself.

GRATITUDE

Angels serve God in gratitude and love. Gratitude opens your heart to receive many blessings from God. Always be grateful even for the little things that you normally take for granted such as all your physical abilities, a good night's sleep, hot water, or even a short queue at the store checkout. Always be grateful not only for the happy moments in your life but also for the sad ones or any situation that arises in your life making you uncomfortable or fearful. They have come to your attention in order to be changed or healed, to help you focus on the positive. To practise the attitude of gratitude, each night before you go to bed think about at least five things that you are grateful for and write them in a gratitude journal.

SURRENDER

Surrender comes with faith. Total faith helps you to walk through closed doors into the unknown, with the trust that you are supported every step of the way. Deep surrender requires relinquishing yourself totally with no expectations or conditions. It could be a frightening process at first, because you are no longer in control, and you may experience a feeling of helplessness and vulnerability. The faith the angels have in God is greater than yours so trust them to hold your hand and walk you through that unknown door. As you learn to surrender, you will fulfil your soul's hunger for Divine love and be filled with love and gratitude.

COMPASSION

Compassion softens your heart. When you are compassionate you are able to see and feel the suffering of others without judgment or criticism. Compassion comes when you transform your own pain and suffering into love. If you are in pain, you are full of anger, or fear and your heart is hardened. This will prevent you from loving yourself. As a result of your hardened heart, you cause pain and suffering to others. Angels inspire you to explore your soul's desires, discover who you are, to find the true parts of yourself. Compassion is having the courage and willingness to listen with an open heart and to find the connection of unconditional love between two souls.

HUMILITY

Humility frees you from all suffering and self deception. Humility is getting in touch with your eternal self and realising your own ignorance and insignificance without which you cannot see your true self. When you are humble, you take full responsibility for your happiness. Your heart and mind is open, you ask, surrender, listen and receive guidance from God and the angels. You do not decide on the outcome are not too proud to say "God, I made a mistake. You are right." You are willing to depart from a position you have held on to. You are more receptive and open to change. Humility brings security. When challenges arise you are able to bend but do not fall like a proud person.

21. ANGEL INVOCATIONS

Angel invocations are heartfelt requests to the angels to help you make personal changes to fulfil your life purpose and to walk your life path in love and light.

FORGIVENESS

Invite archangel Zadkiel - or angel Stamera to help you see the situation from the angelic perspective; to soften your heart and help you forgive yourself and others.

At bedtime give archangel Zadkiel - or angel Stamera permission to come into your dream state and clear away emotional toxins from your heart and mind that you may have consciously or unconsciously accumulated during the day.

Forgiveness heals a hardened heart and frees you from limitations of your mind.

RELATIONSHIP ISSUES

If you are having a difficult relationship with your partner, friend, colleague or family member, which causes you to feel deep anger, call on archangel Uriel to bring his pitcher of amber liquid and to pour it over and into your body, clearing every cell and filling it with love so that you can see the situation from the perspective of love and thus resolve the relationship.

RELEASING ADDICTIONS

To release cravings and addictions, whether they be physical addiction to food, alcohol, drugs and so on or mental negative thought patterns, you must be 100 per cent willing to release the addiction and commit to the process. Go deep within with a heartfelt desire for release, asking Archangel Raphael to help bring to your conscious mind the root cause of your addiction and help you release it.

PHYSICAL ILLNESS

If you are experiencing any physical illness, visualise Archangel Raphael's green blanket covering and healing you while you sleep. If you or a loved one is undergoing surgery, Archangel Raphael will beam his green healing light on the doctors, nurses and everyone involved with the surgery and after-care. For complete healing of the painful areas of surgery, he will also shine this light to act as a balm for healing.

RELEASING CORDS

Cords are something you attach to yourself, to others and can also be attached by others to you. When you curse yourself in anger or frustration you attach cords to these emotions which create a flow of negative energy between you and the emotions, thus bringing stress into your life, and restricting the flow of energy into your chakras. If others are jealous of you or speak to you in anger, or share their fears and worries with you, emotional cords are attached between you both. Each time you or the person to whom this cord is attached feels a negative or positive emotion, this energy flows into you both through this same cord. To release these cords of attachment call on Archangel Michael to cut all negative cords with his sword and to fill the area to which the cord was attached with love.

COSMIC VACUUM
During the day if your thoughts are congested and you feel tired and listless, call on the angels or archangel Michael to bring the cosmic vacuum and clean your thoughts and energy uplifting you to the energy of love. The cosmic vacuum can be used to clear physical surroundings, such as houses, workplaces, hospitals, and so on.

RESURRECTION
Archangel Gabriel is the angel of resurrection and change. Call on Archangel Gabriel to immerse you in the flame of resurrection and free your conscious mind from all limitations, in order to teach you to understand your life path and purpose.

PRAYER FROM KRIAT SH'MA

Repeat this at the start of the day or at night as a form of Divine protection.

"To my right Michael, and to my left Gabriel, in front of me Uriel and behind me Raphael and over my head God's Shekhinah." (The presence of God).

22. ANGELIC ENCOUNTERS

Daughter's fear of Darkness - Ranjini
When at the age of eight my daughter Zoë moved into her own room, she was afraid of the dark and was worried that "bad people" would come into her room through the window. I tried to reassure her that they would need a ladder to reach her window but her fear was so great that she insisted that I leave the corridor light on. At bedtime we asked God for protection. The next day she said to me, "Mum, you don't need to leave the light on any more because a shepherd with a stick and his dog are sitting outside my window." I knew that it was an angel but for my daughter to understand that she was protected, the angel had shown himself as a shepherd.

Protection and healing - Ranjini
Early one morning in September 2007, three weeks before my daughter Zoë was due to start her university education, I had a phone call from her saying she had been in a car accident and was in hospital. I froze when she said the doctors thought she had fractured her spine and squashed a disc. My husband and I rushed to the hospital which was about an hour's drive away. As we drove, to stop my mental chatter and worry, all I could say was "Angels please protect Zoë's spine."

While we were there they placed a "NIL BY MOUTH" board over the bed. This meant that she was due for surgery the next day. I did not want to leave her alone at the hospital but red tape prevented me from staying with her. As I was leaving the hospital I again called on the angels to protect her, be with her and heal her. I also called on Mother Mary to be with Zoë.

On the way home, I was very upset and asked, "How could something like this happen to her, when she was only a passenger in the car? It was unfair that the other three passengers walked away from the accident with only a little bruising." I was very angry and doubting the Divine protection that I ask for daily for me and my family. I could hardly sleep that night worrying about Zoë all alone in hospital.

Early next morning we went back to the hospital we noticed that the NIL BY MOUTH board had been removed. The consultant who came to see Zoë spent hardly a minute by her bedside. I kept asking the angels for some explanation and help. An hour later a junior doctor came along and said that the consultant's opinion was that the fracture was stable and that it would heal on its own. Zoë was fit enough to go home and start her university education. However she had to have fortnightly x-rays to make sure that the disc did not collapse any further. I doubted this diagnosis and I was almost in tears seeing my daughter in so much pain and wondering about the protection and support I had asked for Zoë.

Suddenly the lady in the bed across from Zoë called me. When I walked up to her bedside, very hesitantly she said, "I am a spiritualist and I can see things." I immediately told her that I too had a few friends who were spiritualists. Then she opened up and said that as soon as I had left the ward, she saw Mother Mary come and lie down by Zoë's side and Jesus sitting by her bedside holding her hand. Then a whole host of angels and beings of light, some of whom she didn't recognise, surrounded her bed. Each time Zoë cried in pain she could see Mother Mary stroking her head and whispering into her ear and her crying would cease and she would doze off for a few minutes. This was confirmation to me that my request had been heard and answered.

I was guided to speak to the junior doctor and ask her if arrangements could be made for the x-rays to be done at a different hospital. With reluctance this was arranged and Zoë was transported home by ambulance. My daily mantra was. "Angels, please protect Zoë's spine." After her first x-ray at this hospital she was referred to a spinal consultant who explained to her what would happen if she did not have any operations to mend the fracture. Under his guidance and care, she had two surgeries in 2007 and another in July of 2010. Her bone grafts have taken well and the metal work that was holding up her spine have all now been removed. It was Divine intervention and protection that orchestrated and moved Zoë's care to this consultant. Every day I thank God and the angels for bringing him and his team of doctors and nurses into our lives.

An obligation turns to a life-changing experience - Tamanna Gulati

In 2008, my mom had heard about the angel classes and was very keen to attend. Unfortunately she had fractured her leg in an accident and as a result of this she was unable to be there. She was very disappointed. A few days later she received an invitation from Ranjini from the United Kingdom to attend an angel class. She couldn't believe her eyes when she noticed the address of the venue - it was her home address. We didn't know until much later that it had been arranged by a friend of my sister Hina, and even she didn't know about it until Ranjini arrived in Delhi. (We have lost touch with this friend as he has moved out of Delhi but I know now that he was divinely guided to arrange the class for my Mom).

My sister had attended Ranjini's classes and she suggested that a group class would be more beneficial to my Mom. I was included in this class and I felt an obligation to attend. That was when I came across this wonderful concept of calling on angels for guidance and support. The first minute I met Ranjini I felt so warm and comforted. I don't know how, but I gave myself completely and there was something in me which moved...... it was as if something like popcorn popped in my head. I would never have known that the few hours I spent learning about angels would change my life.

After this session I learnt more about angels and how to call on them for guidance. Whenever I am in doubt, I call on them for help or do an angel reading for myself. I now call on the angels on a daily basis for guidance and support.

Asking for simple things - Pat Rooks

I took my granddaughter to the city centre to shop for some school uniform. As we were entering a parking area I said, out loud "Angels, please find me a convenient parking place." My granddaughter asked what I had said and who was I speaking to. I said that I was speaking to the angels, and, at that moment, I noticed a parking place at the end of the row. She laughed and said that she had told me that there was a space. However, I explained that she wouldn't have seen it if the angels hadn't made it available for us.

Asking for directions - Natasha Thusu

Moving to a new state is fine, but to a new country altogether and finding your way around can be quite unnerving.

My mother accompanied me when I moved to Singapore. As she loves to visit places of spiritual interest and shrines, on a Sunday, we decided to visit the Shrine of Habib Noh, a 19th Century saint and a direct descendant of the Holy Prophet Mohamed, which was located at the other end of Singapore from where I lived. We had no idea how to get there but managed to get to central Singapore on the metro. All the offices were closed, the streets were deserted and central Singapore was like a ghost town and there was only a restricted bus service.

We started walking, as we didn't know our directions, we were lost, my Mom was getting tired and I was losing my patience. At this point I decided to ask Archangel Michael to help me. We came across a pedestrian crossing, when I saw a bus coming on the opposite side, I ran across the road while the light was red, hoping it was the right bus. I asked the driver whether it was going in the direction we wanted to go and he said "yes." Mom and I got into the bus when we noticed we were the only two passengers. My eyes were drawn to the bus route pamphlet. I picked one and started reading it, to my surprise, the bus terminal was called "St Michael's" and the shrine was opposite the terminal. Angels guide us to exactly where need to be irrespective of our religious beliefs.

Blessed with a new job - Hina Gulati
For the past ten years I have been working at the same job and I loved it. However, four years ago the office shifted to another place and as a result it took me 2-3 hours a day travelling to work and back. I felt tired by the time I reached the office and at the end of the day, drained of all energy. At times I did think "Wouldn't it be nice if I could work closer to home, and wished for a better job in terms of opportunity and pay." I did not realise that I was unconsciously asking the angels to manifest a job for me. I looked around for a new job and found one with a newly forming Regional Office of a company based abroad and accepted their offer. I was happy that the journey to the office would only be twenty minutes.

A couple of weeks before I was due to start with the new company, I was informed that they were now looking for office space in a different location, which meant the travelling time would be the same as my previous job and my start date had been postponed indefinitely as the funds for the running of the Indian office was delayed. I was now unemployed and to cover my day to day living expenses for the next three months, I managed to get a loan from a friend to pay my bills and living expenses.

I have immense faith and belief in the angels, specifically with archangel Michael and I have regular chats with him. He's the one I feel connected to most or rather he's the one I feel I can talk to all the time so I keep doing it.

In July an ex-colleague pointed me in the direction of a business opportunity where I could work from home, had a lot of flexibility and the commissions were good. This company is all about helping others to follow their dreams and live a happy and abundant life, which fits in with my dreams. Not only that, this also gave me an opportunity to make my sisters my business partners. And today all three of us are working closely to make each other's dreams come true.

I thank God and Archangel Michael everyday for bringing me this opportunity, especially when I did not have a clue as to how I would begin my professional life.

Taking my power back - Naina

My son was born one month prematurely and after delivery I was given strict instructions by the paediatrician that I should breast-feed for at least six months. I did so but after three months my in-laws pressured me to start his top feed with cows' milk. I consulted my baby's doctor and she told me not to.

At this time I was living with my in-laws and I was going through a bad phase in my life. When I was alone with them or when they had guests they would put me down by saying, that because I was weak (I am short in height and thin of build but that does not make me weak - it's just the way I look) was not producing enough milk to fulfil my baby's demands.

This situation was so stressful and frustrating that I cried a lot because instead of them being supportive, I felt my family was embarrassing me and my motherhood. It seemed to me that even my husband was doubtful whether I could raise our baby.

Instead of looking for support from my husband and family, I decided to stand up for myself and I called upon Archangel Michael to help me so that I could breast feed my baby and stay healthy and stress-free. I made my intention very clear by requesting, "You will take care that I succeed," and had faith and trust that he would help. He did.

In spite of all the odds and everyone doubting my abilities as a mother, and even though my husband did not stand by me, I continued to breastfeed him. He is now fifteen months old and while starting to give him solid foods, I continue to breastfeed him twice a day.

Angels are all around us. They are there to help us. And all we have to do is ask them for help!! Speak it out loud or say it as a silent prayer. Have faith! You will be heard.

So strong is my faith that even my husband and my sister have started believing in angels. As they are still a little doubtful about angelic assistance, when they are faced with an issue that they cannot solve, they come to me and ask me to request Archangel Michael to help them. I am now helping them to build their confidence to ask directly for Archangel Michael's help in whatever situation they encounter.

I have discovered that it is worth giving life a chance when I know there is somebody close to me taking care of me every second of the day. All I have to do is ask for help, for the angels are bound by nature's law never to over-rule our free will. We have to exercise this by asking them to intervene. Most important of all is to be thankful and in gratitude to the angels for their help. They want nothing more from us than just a simple and genuine thank you.

Angels disguised as Policemen - Sahira
Since I started calling on the angels for help, I am aware of many incidents where I could feel their protection, security and presence. When my husband was out of town without knowing why, I took his car and not mine to a party. I

was on my way back at around 2 a.m. when suddenly my car tyre burst on the highway. I was not only travelling alone but I was wearing a mini skirt!!! Everyone knows Delhi can be unsafe and that if a cop tries to stop you after dark, you should try and avoid stopping, especially if you are a girl on your own, as it is believed that harmful things could happen. I was scared.

Suddenly I realised that a voice inside me was saying "Nothing will happen." I immediately called both Archangel Mika'il and Archangel Gabra'il (as I was not sure who I should ask for help). I noticed two policemen approaching me and to my surprise they actually came to protect and help me. These two cops not only changed the tyre but made sure I reached home safe and sound. Many of you might think that this could have been a coincidence. I am sure they were angels disguised as cops, who showed me that cops can be good human beings too. This incident has made me look at cops in a different light.

23. FREQUENTLY ASKED QUESTIONS

How do I ask for help?
Talk to God through prayer, mentally or out loud. All requests for help go to God and He sends His messages via the angels. Once you have asked for help, surrender and wait for the replies without any expectations.

Do you pray to the angels?
Angels are connected to God in love and gratitude and want all the glory to go to God. They do not want us to pray or worship them. You can request their help and have conversations with them. Angels are messengers of God; therefore there is nothing wrong in having a conversation with them.

Can I connect to angels when I am agitated?
God sends additional angels to help you when you are agitated or going through a traumatic. Just say "Angels please help" and you will feel their presence.

If I call on the angels and the other religious deities will they clash?
Angels and other religious deities are all God's messengers of love therefore they will not clash.

I became aware of the angels at the age of 60. Does this mean that the angels were not helping until I started calling on them?
Angels are always watching over you and guiding you towards your life purpose. You may have been asking about your life purpose and angels are making you aware of their presence and guidance that you have been receiving from your birth.

Can I ask for the name of my guardian angel?
Yes you can. Sit quietly, Breathe, relax
Ask question
Be relaxed and wait for response
Name will be repeated over and over again
Name may flash before your eyes
Trust the angel to choose name that will resonate with you.

Do I need to go through an attunement process to communicate with the angels?
You are connected to God and the angels through every breath that you take. Therefore you do not need an attunement to communicate with the angels. In chapter 14 I discuss how to develop your intuitive skills to be aware of angelic communication.

What is the angels' opinion on bargaining?
Bargaining is a human concept; therefore you do not have to bargain with God or the angels. Trust God to provide you with all your needs and desires. Everything is given to you according to God's will.

I hope you enjoy your journey with the angels and may they shower God's love and blessings upon you.

Ranjini Woodhouse
www.souljourney.co.uk

Lightning Source UK Ltd.
Milton Keynes UK
UKOW02f1341131014

240028UK00002B/7/P